DREAMS, VISIONS, *and* DESTINY

God's View Surpasses Worldview for Everyday Living

Paula Yolandé Wilson, Ph.D.

WestBow Press books may be ordered through booksellers or by contacting:

WestBow Press
A Division of Thomas Nelson & Zondervan
1663 Liberty Drive
Bloomington, IN 47403
www.westbowpress.com
844-714-3454

ISBN: 979-8-3850-3461-1 (sc)
ISBN: 979-8-3850-3462-8 (e)

Library of Congress Control Number: 2024920425

Print information available on the last page.

WestBow Press rev. date: 09/28/2024

To my daughters, Angela and Juanita, and her family, Paul (her husband), Whitney, Paige, and Kobe (my grandchildren). Family is an inspiration and a way to understand the spiritual legacy of our heritage. To my wonderful friends who I have known more than twenty years, you have stuck with me and helped me grow into the person I am today.

Contents

Introduction

On the left bicep, there was a beautiful flower. It was flowing like a stream, charming and rustling in the wilderness. The flower was growing toward the upturned palm of the dreamer's hand. The green stem was brightly emerging from the bicep. Then, growing slowly and astonishingly, there were colorful bluish-purple petals with a wavy pattern. As the petals grew, they expanded out of the green stem to a full bloom. A rich bright yellow started to appear as the flower grew. The yellow teardrop shape appeared in the center of the bluish-purple petal. A white line trimmed the yellow teardrop as the flower grew and exposed the inner beauty.

The arm was at a forty-five-degree angle, and the bicep was bulging on the woman's arm. As she looked around, she became aware of a bathroom. Looking at a door to the left of the flower, her sister was peering into the room. It was pitch-black behind the dreamer's sister. The lighting in the bathroom was amber. Straight ahead, a strange man was looking at the flower. When the man looked at the flower, it began to recede halfway back into the arm.

This dream was the inspiration for writing about dreams and dream interpretations. The flower in the dream is a fleur-de-lis. The growth stages represent growth and strength. From a religious viewpoint, the fleur-de-lis is identified as God the Father, God the Son, and God the Holy Spirit.[1] They are synchronized and in unison with each other.[2]

Humanity is defined by emotional and mental control. Historically, the symbol was used in the Louisiana Purchase territory as a brand on the bodies of slaves.[3] The flower symbol was also a control object on the slaves to keep them from fleeing. Branding was a form of mental and emotional control as well as identifying physical property.

Freedom through our emotional health and thoughts help us to be our own selves and who God meant us to be. Today, we are free from the branding

---

[1] Genesis 1:1–2 (NLT).
[2] Cirlot 2001, 1971, 1962.
[3] Branam 2023.

(ownership of our humanity as less than human beings) and can stand our ground in victory. Mental and physical control can have a hold on someone and make them think they are less than human. They are treated as insignificant, and they don't feel a sense of belonging. Mental and emotional bondage are still prevalent in American society.

We can view ourselves from the inside out. Dreams are images in our minds as well as our thoughts[4] on a subconscious level. They are thoughts while we are asleep. Some psychologists call dreams hallucinations. Dreams are more than meaningless hallucinations that conjure up perceptions in our thoughts and provide something illusionary.[5] They are "uniquely crafted imagery that is related symbolically to feelings"[6] and emotions. These feelings and emotions are unique to each individual and their everyday living circumstances.

We can open our eyes and see while they are closed in sleep. Many cultures today lack any awareness of the significance of dreaming. In some cultures, the lack could be due to their contemporary lifestyles that prioritizes productivity, material success, and rational thinking over understanding the value of the subconscious or inner selves. The focus of this book is

---

[4] Hamon 2000, Murphy 2008.

[5] Domhoff 2018, 357.

[6] Ullman 1990, 123.

to understand how God still speaks to us today through dreams and visions. God gives dreams and visions to men and women and boys and girls.[7] He speaks to believers of his Gospel today as well as those in the past though dreams, visions, supernatural activities, and prophesies.[8] This concept is from Christian beliefs and the notion that God is universal. God is universal, and the "nature and meaning of dreams come from the humanities."[9] Dreams help us understand who we are in relation to other humans individually, locally, and globally. It provides an understanding of how we fit into society. Our belief in God expands our place in society and is based on a spiritual point of view. This book searches deeper into dreams and their guidance from God and his Holy Spirit.

God is answering our prayers, and we can listen and see what he has to say. Dreaming, from a scientific point of view, occurs during the REM and non-REM stages of sleep. This is not the focal point of this book. It is not an emphasis from a psychological or scientific perspective. Research shows us how God speaks to us through dreams.[10]

---

[7] Hamon 2000, Flanagan 2000.

[8] Prince 1993, 37.

[9] Flanagan 2000, 4.

[10] Hamon 2000, Riffel 1993, Gilbert 1985, Flanagan 2000.

Don't overreact. We can know on a conscious level what the subconscious has to say. The book is not meant to provide commercial "cult culture."[11] It is not presenting solutions to individual problems. Everyone must take responsibility for their own interpretations and understandings of their dreams. Interpretations of individual dreams are based on cultural beliefs. Some people have issues and dreams that require more help than this book cannot produce. Therapy is acceptable. Trust God during life's journey. It is fine to get professional, emotional, and mental help when needed.[12]

Secrets are revealed in people's hearts. Whether scandalous or not, dreams are universal. They come to believers and nonbelievers of God. Only the God of all gods knows the secrets in people's hearts, and he reveals the truths of dreams through interpretations.[13] Dreams and visions help shape our destinies and prepare our hearts and minds (listening ears) for the blessing of God to manifest his promises. When we understand our dreams and visions, we understand our life experiences and the purpose of our dreams and visions. People can gain confidence when they understand that dreams provide direction and guidance toward their destinies.

[11] Ullman 1990.

[12] Krippner 1990, 123.

[13] Daniel 2:27–30 (NLT).

Fear not because the truth will be revealed. Universal propaganda is used to instill fear in people from different cultures and races. Love is the opposite of fear. It is powerful and can eliminate negativity. Cruel and brutal hearts and minds propagate fear in "Christians." In the United States, this fear is based on Caucasian and European ideologies that have been assimilated into modern society.

Unity can be revealed through opening our hearts and minds to the truth. Christian Europeans deconstructed African identities to keep them obedient and beneath their constructed society. The removal of race from the hearts and minds of people can lead to reconstructed racial identities. Eliminating the race factor allows for unity and equality in resources.

Put fences up to keep the enemy out, and open the gates of our hearts to let love in. Our thoughts, emotional intelligence, and faith determine our destinies. God sets up boundaries and guidance for successful lives in his glory. Boundaries must be established and directed toward friends, family, and neighbors to keep them from overstepping in our relationships. They can intentionally or unintentionally interfere in the process of growing closer to the ones we love.

Sleep and dreams are essential for well-being[14] of an individual, a family, a home, and a work environment. Visions are manifest on a conscious or subconscious level and are different from dreams. They are also manifested by God as being one and the same as dreams.

[14] Murphy 2008.

CHAPTER 1

Dreams Are the Life Energy of God

A Dream of God's Call in England in the Nineties

She was preaching on a busy intersection, and the crowds of people were ignoring her. She was preaching the Word of God to anyone who would listen. She was embarrassed because she did not believe it was the correct way of speaking about God. The people were going around her and ignoring her oration. An overwhelming feeling of shame came over her, and then the dream transitioned.

Everyone was preparing to go out and evangelize in Lancaster, England. It was a group of ministers and laypeople. The bus was preparing to leave, and the people were boarding. One of the ministers wore a black sweater with a red crackle design. It was her turn to preach on the street as she had seen the ministers before her preaching. Once she opened her mouth, the Word of God came flowing out of her with ease. The crowds on the busy intersection began to circle around her, watching and listening as she preached the Word of God.

When God Speaks, Listen Carefully.

Dreams and visions are God's iconographic voice. "God speaks to believers and unbelievers alike through dreams and visions."[15] They are a deeper way of allowing God to speak to our innermost being. Understanding what God is saying to us in our dreams and visions is vital to our mental and emotional well-being.

Keep Following the Intuition of the Heart—and We Will Thrive[16]

Dreams are images in our minds and our subconscious thoughts.[17] They are our thoughts while we're asleep. They are also a representation of a symbolic reality rather than hallucinations that invoke a perception

---

15 Riffel 1993, 6.
16 Proverbs 13:19 (NLT).
17 Hamon 2000, Murphy 2008.

in our thoughts and provide something illusionary.[18] They are also "uniquely crafted imagery that is related symbolically to feelings"[19] and emotions. These feelings and emotions are exclusive to an individual and their everyday circumstances.

Don't Be in Denial—Love Is Revealed through Dreams

Why do people need to understand their destinies through their dreams and visions? Understanding the distinction between God's view and the world's view is significant if we are to grow in maturity and understand that reality and the spirit world are relevant. It is crucial to recognize that God is represented as three persons: Father, Son, and Holy Spirit. Their voice is one. The powerful, thunderous voice, whether loud or softly spoken, is one because they are one.[20] The Father's voice bears witness to his Son, Jesus. Understanding this concept helps us understand the work of the Holy Spirit in the lives of everyone.[21] God relates to us mostly symbolically in dreams and visions to reveal Himself[22]

---

[18] Domhoff 2018, 357.
[19] Ullman 1990, 123.
[20] John 5:37 (NLT).
[21] John 6:46, 14:7–9 (NLT).
[22] Gilbert 1985, 7, Riffel 1993.

and his heart's desire in us. Most dreams are symbolic and must be deciphered to get to the truth of what the dream is telling us. "Through dreams, God is seeking to bring us into wholeness and balance."[23]

Open Our Eyes and Listen as We Sleep

Some dreams are direct guidance to follow and have symbols of direction and clarity that cannot be denied. The dream in England came to the dreamer when the Gospel Inspirational Fellowship Church went out on the street to preach in the nineties. The American-led nondenominational church was developed by military personnel in Bicester, England.[24] It evolved from the Gospel service on the base and transitioned to the local community.

Don't Crash and Burn—Trust God

Dreamers are not immune to the trials and sufferings of the devil. He will use the people close to us to inflict despair and try to destroy or delay what God has designed for our lives. Have you ever been to church with your family, and as soon as you leave church, your

[23] Riffel 1993, 93.

[24] Upper Heyford AFB, England.

companion finds something petty to pick a fight about? As you sit in the car and wonder what just happened, the argument escalates to a loud verbal, or possibly physical, altercation. The space is small, and there is nowhere to go in a moving car with an angry person. You feel trapped with nowhere to go, confusion sets in, and your sentiments must be held in check to keep from escalating the rage. We are not responsible for the emotions of others, but we can react in a way that prevents them from overpowering our inner urges to reply with the same energy.

Inner Disposition Is Greater Than an Ungodly Response

Quietness is the best reaction at the time, based on emotions and personality, as we try to figure out why our loved one is distressed and unhappy. The children in the back seat are shocked and surprised. They are staring at the front seat and wondering what will happen next. Everyone is wondering, *What just happened?* Emotional, mental, and physical abuse are common in the church environment as well as among those who do not worship in a community.

These emotional issues did not stop the dreamer from dreaming. It diverted her focus and attention away from the emotional distress her partner was creating in the family and onto the protection of her children. The children were the focus because God advises us to train up children the way they should go, and when they get old, they will not depart from the way.

The need to protect the children is multiplied due to concerns about them not getting the proper protection from the ones who love them. We do not want our children to grow up learning how to resolve issues by witnessing their loved ones' immature conflict resolution. It's not wise to allow children to witness arguments. The actions and angry words portrayed in front of them translate mentally and emotionally. It is likely they will grow up understanding that people can consistently talk to them with discontent and anger.

The Devil Sits Outside the Church, Waiting to Pick a Fight

We just came from church. This fight has a far-reaching negative effect because the young minds think the household efforts of going to church created the chaos. Words can bring life or kill a person's soul. Perceptive training in the hearts and minds of children allows a person to speak to them in a condescending way. Visual perception and acuity through listening are life's teaching tools and translate to striking images for their mental and emotional issues.

Human Dignity Is So Important

What's happening is a learned way to resolve conflict, and it is a practical message. The issues aren't really resolved in this way, and the adults have emotional and psychological trauma. It is a temporary device to strike out at something tangible for an intangible problem. Numerous scriptures in the Bible let a person know how to treat their partners and children. If they are not abiding by the Word of God, the family could become troublesome. This can lead to confrontations and an opening for spiritual attacks. Direct communication with God through prayer will provide protection. Prayer is needed to cover everyone, including the broken person who is struggling with their own emotional and mental issues. As we consciously try to live godly lives through meekness and quietness, we can resist rendering evil for evil and overcome the flesh of retaliation.

The dreamer's nature and personality are quiet and loving during any conflict. She grew up with multiple siblings and rarely saw her parents fighting. Her mother never used a swear word in front of the children. We must be thoughtful about the words that flow out our mouths. Trusting in the Holy Spirit to bridle our tongues takes a lot of restraint. The "well of life," the mouth, manifests our inner convictions, beliefs, and values. When we are sleeping, and the subconscious is showing us the mysteries of our hearts through dreams, we are victorious. The victory is manifest through acting on our beliefs and hoping for a better present and future. The inner person is the fountainhead, and the heart is the spring. That doesn't mean that everything is utopian—and there are no nightmares or bad dreams. Dreams reveal the good and bad to a person so that they can meditate on the meanings and get an interpretation for a better understanding.

There was a time when God was answering the dreamer's prayers through direct communication. "I shall not die but live to declare the works of the Lord" was her motto in life. As she was going to sleep one night, the thunderous voice of God spoke loudly over her. Her eyelids had almost closed when she heard the shout. As her head hit the pillow, she heard one word from the heavens. It came at the moment she was going into a sleep state to rest her body and soul. The word was spoken in an unknown tongue. It wasn't understood by her, but the power that came behind it into the depths of her soul was heard and felt at the same time. She went to sleep in peace.

Just Take a Deep Breath and Breathe

Dreams are the breath of God. The breath of God brings life, and Jesus is the great I Am. He brings life to our dreams through the Holy Spirit, revealing dreams to us and providing interpretations of the dreams so that we can boldly go forward with our beliefs and faith. Even though the powerful spoken word to the dreamer wasn't understood, it agreed with the written word in the spirit and soul of her heart.

God intimately speaks and communes with our innermost being through our faith and trust in Him. It is personally and confidentially connected to each of us. It is the calm during the storm that is raging inside, and it gives us an escape from the many storms of life.

Walking or running, we are still moving toward our destiny. Home should be a place to live joyfully and peacefully. When others around us are in turmoil, we can quietly meditate on God and patiently wait on him for a change or a way to escape. Choose to love God and seek him for an understanding of our dreams and visions. These dreams and understandings are due to discerning that they are from God. In doing so, we can journey toward our destinies in a better environment than psychological hostilities and emotional distress from our loved ones.

If we obey the voice of God when it is spoken through dreams and visions, our belief and faith help us cling to what is given to our souls as a promise that will come to pass. Make the decision and plan to escape a bad situation that has gone on for years. That doesn't mean giving up on someone who is having a difficult time loving their family. A person knows how much they can tolerate from another human being. Sticking around beyond that tolerance is futile and opens a door for loss of life, whether spiritually or physically. God will give us the peace we need for self-care. Everything will be all right, and we won't become casualties of spiritual and/or natural warfare. Friction in relationships can sap our vitality. We will speak in more detail about relationship abrasions and how our dreams can bring harmony in a later chapter.

In our dreams, the surreptitious things of God are revealed to us through his Holy Spirit. His Spirit speaks to our spirit and brings hope through the agreement of his spoken Word, written Word, and faith. Our faith in that hope brings the manifestation of God's blessings into reality. Soak up the life energy of God by recognizing that dreams are meant to help and bring no harm. Fear is the opposite of faith, and it feeds pride.

CHAPTER 2

Humbleness is Contrary to Pride

Pride goes before the fall—and how the mighty fall hard. Humbleness allows a person to be set free from mental and emotional bondage. Dreams give blessings and warnings that lead us to our final destiny of life. Our thoughts are not God's thoughts until he shares them with us and gives us an expected end. His thoughts are not evil and will not guide us to do evil things.[25] Our hearts need to be adjusted for our minds to come in line with God's thoughts. Once we have an idea of what God's plan is, it's imperative that we do not deviate from his direction and go off on our own, which pride will tempt a person to do.

Stop blaming God—and start listening to what he

[25] Jeremiah 29:11 (KJV), Riffel 1993, 20.

has to say. Don't complain when we are going through traumatic and unbearable incidents in life. These issues will pass, and we will come out on the other end as better people than when we started. Complaining is an attribute that is hard to overcome because it is used as a tool for getting to a favorable place in life. These happy places might be at home, on the job, or in family environments.

John C. Maxwell's *How Successful People Think* states, "Thinking is a discipline—act on good thought."[26] Success comes from getting control of our thoughts and disciplining them to root out the negative ones. Our actions test the spirit to see if it's of God.[27] If the dream doesn't come to pass, it was not from God. It was self-gratification and wanting. We can have desires that are immoral and not of God's direction. Interpretations should lead to life and not to destruction. Destruction comes from our imperfect inner selves. Perfection comes from God living in our hearts. It's the heart of man that results in the consequences of their actions motivated by their principles. When we are assured, our good thoughts overpower negativity.

People go through things in life that perplex them. They are tempted to blame God for their tragedies. We

---

[26] Maxwell 2009.

[27] Deuteronomy 18:20.

can turn things around as we are going through them. Elihu, Job's friend, argued that Job did not hear God speaking because of his pride and lack of humility. Job was not being humble and took his complaint to God in prayer. He asked why he was going through such events while he claimed to be a staunch religious person who adored Him.

We might consider ourselves staunch Christians, but that does not exclude us from distressing events. The point Elihu brought up is still important today. He believed that Job wasn't listening to God because of his complaints. He adamantly believed God "speaks again and again, though people do not recognize it. He speaks in dreams, in visions of the night, when deep sleep falls on people as they lie in their beds. He whispers in their ears."[28] Even in the difficult times where we are wrestling with a complaining spirit, give that spirit over to God and be humble.

Speak life and not death over our souls. It's important to speak scriptures over our lives daily to overcome negative thoughts. Ask God for deliverance from chaotic thoughts and the voices in our minds and believe that he has delivered us. The random thoughts that are trying to overwhelm us will flee. Try to recognize spiritual

---

[28] Job 33:14–16b (NLT).

warfare of the mind, body, and soul.[29] Cast our cares on Jesus before going to sleep every night—and trust God to watch over us while we sleep.

The outhouse was the size of a modern-day port-a-potty. It was wooden and worn. The wood was dingy and brown. There was no smell, but the dreamer ran into the outhouse and closed the door. She was concerned about doing the right thing in taking care of her family. Would she be able to protect them from the enemy that was trying to destroy them? Would she be able to continue to do God's work as they transitioned back to the United States? It was dark in the outhouse, and when she came out, she saw a racetrack.

The track had pristine white lines for everyone to stay in their lanes. Men and women and boys and girls were preparing for a race. When the gun went off, she ran as fast as she could. She came in third place, but she felt like she had earned a trophy. She immediately demanded her trophy from the man who stood in front of her. As she was reaching for the trophy, the man pulled the trophy back toward his shoulder and said, "The trophy is not for you to demand. It is for me to give." He was dressed in a bright white toga. His skin was bronze, and his face was obscure.

We're already winners, but God gives the crown of

[29] Murphy 2008.

life. The dreamer was in the middle of transitioning back to the United States from an overseas military tour in England with her spouse and children. Military families have always endured many emotional, mental, and physical challenges. The families must pack up and move every few years. The stress from the military member affects the family when it comes to handling the changes that must be made. If the family does not have a solid foundation—or if any emotional or psychological cracks have not been addressed—the fissures will widen and eventually cause destruction. Those cracks could even be relationship problems.

Unresolved issues in the past cause cracks and destruction in a relationship. The relationship problems might be a spouse trying to fix everything on their own. Perhaps they might not be trying to fix the problems at all. The problem might be ignored because of a lack of understanding of how to resolve it and heal the family. Everyone is embarrassed and thinks the problems will go away on their own.

When two people come together as a family, they might come from different societies, cultures, or beliefs. If they don't understand how the other person grew up with different beliefs and values, there could be clashes and challenges. A man might believe he should raise his family the way he was raised and follow in his father's footsteps in how he treats the women in his family. His father might be his idol. He thinks that is how a man shows he is a man. He loves him dearly and thinks of him as an example of how a father is supposed to be. If his father was harsh to his mother, the son will be harsh to the women he encounters and think it's acceptable behavior. Each person can make changes within themselves. The church can provide guidance. No church should guide a person to stay with someone who is so aggressive that it overcomes the other persons will and destiny for their life. The conflict leads to internal hostilities which leads to destruction of one person over the other. Don't bring past issues into a new relationship.

The dreamer wants to manage her family according to her beliefs, values, and upbringing. God is a part of her family dynamic, and she worries that the clashes with her husband will hinder her growing in God's anointing. She is loyal to her husband, children, and church family because she loves God—and she loves them. The struggle is real. Be humble. Someone who is not happy in life might take out their unhappiness on the people who are closest to them. The dreamer is concerned about the health and welfare of her loved ones. Maybe the broken person is speaking to someone in the church. Maybe they can speak with someone at work about their overwhelming urges and disappointments in life.

What will make us happy? It is not healthy to be with someone who is consistently unhappy as a partner. It's imperative to have strong communication and resolve problems together. Selfishness and pride must be eliminated as much as possible. The lack of leadership of a family due to past failures or multiple partners before the marriage can lead to an emotional and psychological break. It is important to move past hostilities—despite what traditionalists in the church believe. Unless someone humbles themselves and get help, it is futile to fight against their emotional and psychological issues.

Silence is not a virtue here, but it gives us a chance to think and hear from God on our own terms. Quietness and meekness are not weakness. Love can overcome the hostilities from the people they hurt the most. The heart of man can become obstinate toward his mate, and it can be difficult to come back from years of hostilities. A person must understand unconditional love. If we love someone dearly, it does not mean we must live with the harshness in their heart. It might be wiser to part ways.

It's difficult to move on when someone has children who depend on a stable family environment. Boundaries must be established for survival and success. Callousness can set in due to stubbornness and pride. It took several years of fighting and bickering in front of the children—and the attacks on the mental health and well-being of others—to decide it was time to let go and move on.

Nostalgia is necessary, but it is not king. There are happy times when the family is visiting museums and amusement parks, which relieves stress. They have fun and try to bond emotionally and physically. Going to baseball games can be nostalgic and a way of bringing memories into a family. Thinking about how we were brought up and our successes can feel euphoric.

Sleep is essential for rejuvenation of the body, mind, and soul. A nostalgic spirit looks to the past, but we must endure and be humble. Let go of past hurts, harms, and tragedies and move toward the future.[30] Forgive yourself for allowing those actions to paralyze you—and look toward the future and the destiny that God has revealed. God's seamless end is life and not death or destruction. The awesome spiritual life starts with believing in God's Son, Jesus, who he sent to this earth for redemption of our sins.

Renewing our hearts and minds brings us back to God's intimacy. Sin separates us from God, and his redemption is a way to reconnect with God. He is all-powerful, all-knowing, and everywhere at all times.

[30] Murphy 2008.

Dreams and visions bring us back to him in an intimate place and time, and we can connect and understand ourselves. Humility helps us open our hearts and minds to hear what God is telling us through our dreams and visions. We can get to a place of humility by opening our hearts to receive the truth. Our ears are telling us how to react to life's challenges.

When we are speaking about things that we are unhappy about, instead of focusing on the expected end, we can get distracted. These distractions can take us down a path that is not where we should be going, which makes it harder to turn around and find the correct path. When we speak about what is making us unhappy, we must find a solution to get us back on track.

Get back in the race. Get back on track for life's journey. Focusing on what God has shown us through dreams and gaining an understanding of his revelations will get us back on the right path. His voice will provide an opportunity to hear more of where he is leading us. A quiet soul is one that hears clearly because it's taking the time to listen and understand what is being said. It's important to listen to a voice we are familiar with and not a strange one because not all voices are of God.

CHAPTER 3

Dreams and Visions are Symbols of Direction and Clarity

Dreams provide intuitive guidance. The dreamer was a layperson who handed out Gospel pamphlets and spoke to anyone who would stop and listen. The people who were stopping to listen were interested in the subject of the preaching experience.

As the ministerial group was preparing for its trip to Lancaster, a minister showed up in a black sweater with a red crackle design. The dream came to pass. The dreamer intuitively believed that God was calling her to the ministry, and that gave her the confidence to step out and do what he was asking her to do.

Human nature exposed faith over fear. The dreamer was a meek and quiet introvert. She was very shy. The first part of the dream indicated that if she got out there on her own, she would be embarrassed. The second part of the dream showed that if she began preaching under the anointing of God, the Holy Spirit would be speaking through her and lifting the name of Jesus. This nugget of knowledge never ends, and we can use it in any situation we go through.

Trusting God is the key. He has shown us the positive parts of moving forward and doing things. We will be successful if we do something he has guided us to do. If we step out and do something God has not guided us to do, and move in our own selfishness, we will get embarrassed. Fear and selfishness prompt us to do the opposite of what God has shown us. God, speaking through us as we operate in his calling and destiny, will draw people to accept Jesus as the Lord and Savior of our sins.

Our testimonies magnify our actions. Once the dreamer finished evangelizing in Lancaster, she rushed over to a friend's house. The friend is wife of the minister who also wore the sweater with the red crackle design. She asked her friend why her husband had worn the sweater that day. His wife stated that he was going to wear something else, but she went into a drawer where his clothes were, pulled out the sweater, and told him to wear it instead. He agreed.

God uses people in different ways to develop and

confirm his calling and direction for our lives. These people were in the dreamer's innermost social circle. Although we usually develop very special friends, upon moving to other locations, we might be reluctant to develop a social circle because of previous obligations or travel. We develop superficial friends who like to keep us at arm's length. A person doesn't always recognize that a friend has kept them around as an acquaintance instead of a close friend. This issue is probably due to differences in beliefs, values, living experiences, or locations. They probably keep us around for information they might get from us on a professional or personal level or to overcome the obstacles they might be encountering. These relationships are usually started for commercial or financial gain. The relationship is more transactional instead of sharpening each other and becoming more transformational in life.

Hang on to the "golden" friends no matter what the time and distance. Social circles evolve over time. We can reconnect with old friends and develop closer relationships by keeping up with significant events in each other's lives. We might be stationed where other people have settled down after their military obligations. We can unite with folks we have known in the church or persons we have had bonds with during our travels. We can share our hopes and dreams and explain how they have come to pass or evolved over the years.

Each person's history brings certain dreams to fruition. Social interactions, connections, empathy, being partial to the emotions that dreams bring to us when God has directly spoken to us can bring clarity.

Know and grow through the process of understanding dreams. A person must believe that it is more than their imagination and meaningless manifestations that conjured up the dreams in their subconscious. If they believe their dreams are too symbolic to understand, they might subconsciously forget them or disregard them in a rational way.[31] The symbols manifested in the subconscious mind will be developed as a person matures in their beliefs and trusts in God's revelation of the symbols in their awakened life.[32] An assumption of scholars is that "dreams are a creation of the dreamer."[33] If we are believers and know that we are recreated in Jesus's image, then the creation of our dreams is of God and the Holy Spirit within us. Whether good or bad, dreams are healing from the inside out.[34]

Paralyzed people, take up your bed and walk. There

---

[31] Hamon 2000.
[32] Ibid.
[33] Cushway 1992.
[34] Cushway 1992.

are often events in our lives where we look for clarity in our thoughts and examine how they hinder us or paralyze us. The emotional and mental bondage from moving toward our future and dreams are released through faith in knowing that the Holy Spirit is guiding us symbolically through our dreams. In *Sleep, Dreaming, and Memory,* scholars agree that "dreaming is one event that is largely independent of ordinary environmental stimuli."[35] They explain the significance of dreaming and the personal nature of the dream being individually developed.

Dreams have cultural functions outside scientific theory and psychology. These cultural functions are proven through religious and healing ceremonies and are used by people who believe in these cultural ideas.[36] The Bible stresses the significance of managing our thoughts from God's perspective. This perspective lets the Word of God dominate our lives, including the "it is written" impression Jesus provided to resist the devil and destructive thoughts.[37]

When the Word of God and his Spirit line up with our faith and beliefs, the creative authority of dreams belongs to God and provides guidance and truth

[35] Fox and Christoff 2018, 327.

[36] Domhoff 2018, 366.

[37] John 10:34, Luke 4:12, Romans 8:5–6 (NLT).

through his dominance and power.[38] We cannot have one without the other concerning the Word and the Spirit of God. The sinful nature that drove a person before they started letting the Spirit of God control their life and thoughts will become a struggle. When the struggle tries to arise, remember that God is not the author of confusion. If confusion tries to set in, ask God through prayer to provide truth and make clear the dream. Dream interpretation has layers and will be discussed more in later chapters.

Prayer brings freedom to mental bondage. Shaping our lives in prayer will provide victory over mental warfare.[39] The Holy Spirit provides emotional passion through the groaning and utterances that cannot be expressed in words to the Father in heaven. God knows our hearts and our weaknesses and understands what the Holy Spirit is saying to him through our human nature. The intensity of praying with emotional faith connects us and gives us the strength to continue in our unwavering faith and never give up. Dreams come to pass in God's time, which is not the same as the timeline and boundaries set up for humans to follow on this earth.

Being quiet is an action that speaks louder than

---

[38] Prince 1993.

[39] Hinson 1988.

words. Find a quiet place for meditation, study the Bible, and seek translucency. Review the questions in our minds that are causing confusion. Eliminate the threats and praise through the silence of waiting on a response from God for interpretation of the symbols in our dreams. Doing this will overcome the limitations we have put on our minds that rob us of the miracle God is attempting to provide. Our hearts and minds must be one with God to overcome the hurdles.

CHAPTER 4

Don't Limit the God Within and the Unction of the Holy Spirit

The Judeo-Christian worldview is based on symbolic thinking. Symbolic language is global, and ancient vestiges have proven them to be a vital part of many cultures and societies. Miracles are still valid today, and many are recorded in the Bible. Life is very busy, and if we are too busy to take quiet time to reflect on what is going on in our lives, we will miss out on what God is saying to us in our dreams and visions.

Overcome universal propaganda. We miss out due to the circumstances happening in our lives in a chaotic manner. It is essential to double down against the negativity of social media, the internet, and electronic media. It is information overload. Negativity limits growth. The world thrives on cruelty and negativity.

That doesn't mean it is not going to attack and drag us down to the valley of worries and anxiety. Just know hopes and dreams shall live.[40]

Emotions create other good thoughts. God has given us a promise and guidance in our dreams, and that drives our faith to manifest it to reality. Time does not manage the space God has given us to bring the dream to pass. It will come to pass whether we hang onto the dream or not. We must "feed the process and create mental momentum."[41]

Keep believing in your dreams and repeating the messages against doubt and fear. Make a habit of believing in your dreams and admonish the negative thoughts. We must identify where our thoughts are coming from. Once we realize where they are coming from, we can overcome with the help of God. The Word of God combats negativity. It's essential to store up the Word of God in our hearts and minds. We can limit God and the Holy Spirit with our thoughts and minds, which drives our hearts to the lives we believe we can inhabit.

The majority of what is provided and narrated today through social media, the internet and electronic media are linear logic and the opinions of everyone without

[40] Ezekiel 37:4–7 (NLT).

[41] Maxwell 2009.

consciousness of others.[42] It is based on self-reliance and opinion in an addictive manner. The addictive manner is mostly narrated on a commercial level for consumerism. These products and their success teach alternative beliefs rather than belief in God.

Worry versus Faith

Make the right choice. Beliefs rooted in superstition will show up on a subconscious level as we go to sleep with worries in our minds. Worry will show up in our dreams and manifest itself as chaos, which causes us not to change. Worry is fear. Fear limits the direction God is trying to get us to go without forcing the issue. We are always free to make the right choices in our lives. We don't make the right choices all the time. We make our choices out of ignorance or without understanding that obstacles can hinder our choices. Making the right choices comes from trusting in what God has shown us through our dreams and visions and acting on the Word of God in our hearts.

The devil doesn't want us to be successful in our work for God and in our lives. It's imperative to consistently study the Bible. Studying the Bible consistently provides knowledge and understanding to overcome obstacles

[42] Batterson 2016, 52, Gilbert 1985, 12.

that will try to block what the devil thinks God is doing in our lives. The knowledge God provides in our dreams and visions is solid because it is based on the Word of God. Satan does not understand what God has assigned to us. He sets up strategies that try to counter what God has planned for our lives.

Understanding spiritual warfare and how to overcome obstacles is vital for success. Ask the Holy Spirit of God for the wisdom and knowledge to understand what is to be applied to us. God gives us the big picture of the dream and visions so that we have the freedom to pursue the value and lesson of the dream. It gives us freedom to create the details through translating the symbols to the vision or dream, which gives us the power to move forward with what God is calling us to do.[43] The greatest belief is that big-picture dreamers are intuitive.

We know the truth, and we know it will set us free. God challenges us to understand more. He answered Job's complaints with rhetorical questions. In Job 38:36, God said, "Who hath put wisdom in the inward parts? Or who hath given understanding to the heart?"

Dreams and visions reveal the treasure of intuition. This intuition is an internal power that provides wisdom and understanding within ourselves. People often say,

---

[43] Maxwell 2009, 35.

"I have a gut feeling." This intuitive feeling reveals our belief and faith, which bring our dreams to pass. This belief and faith in what we dream will manifest on a conscious level what our subconscious is trying to bring into reality.

God created the universe and the dreams within us. Stay a humble person, and God will reveal this secret treasure. The truth is that dreams "are messages sent either from God's Spirit or from our own soul, that comprises our mind, will, and emotions."[44] This will help bring light to the interpretation. They help us focus on the goals we are striving for success. The subconscious can provide a resolution to a problem that is confronting us during the dream. It's on time to reflect what our souls are trying to tell us. We can overcome the immoral nature within and do the right thing.

Dreams are more than a vision or a plan. They are the direction for which the Holy Spirit is guiding us, and they are significant for growth. This guidance represents God's voice and leads to manifesting the vision and plan for our lives. Our dreams will manifest in the subconscious mind,[45] and the symbols are personal to us.

---

[44] Hamon 2000, 24.

[45] Ibid.

Faith Shaken but Overcome by Trust

Once God uses our dreams to reveal how our direction and goals will manifest itself in us, we must stay focused. We must stand strong in our beliefs and in faith until the dream comes to pass—regardless of what happens. Don't let anyone shake your faith or trust in God. Pastor Nicole Crank said, "Be intentional about your goals."[46] This is God's powerful advice for moving forward—no matter what obstacles stand in the way.

We must do something beneficial. Forgiveness releases us from mental and emotional captivity. When people don't care about the destinies God has set for their lives, they will hurt people. They won't fully understand that what they have done is a result of their reaction to the person's dreams that was revealed to them personally.[47]

Dreams are not the end of a person's destiny. They are about future successes. If we haven't moved past these destructive people, we must adhere to his boundaries so that the dreams and visions God gives us can manifest in our lives in God's time.

---

[46] Crank 2020, 70.

[47] Luke 23:34.

Betrayal Revealed

Judas was one of Jesus's disciples, but he didn't have the vision until after he betrayed Jesus. He was focusing on the law of the land and material gain from knowing Him.[48] His financial transaction of receiving silver from Jesus's haters for inside information on his inner circle of friends and whereabouts proved his level of fellowship.

Some people hover around us to see what they can get from us or for status and networking. They use our blessings in our lives for their gain. Judas also thought it was wasteful of Mary when she washed Jesus's feet with expensive oil and anointed him with the essence of nard.[49] This oil could have been sold for money and better living conditions, which he desired to obtain.

When we commune and fellowship through eating with Jesus, it's never a foolish action. We should worship and praise God with the resources we have available. Judas constantly complained of material waste, missing the relevance of the fulfillment of God's promise in his presence. As one of Jesus's disciples, he didn't have a vision of the kingdom of God and his power over earthly things until after the betrayal and his death.[50]

---

[48] Franklin 2018.

[49] John 12:3–6, Franklin 2018.

[50] Acts 1:16–19.

Jesus is in each person who has accepted his provision for salvation. Hold firmly onto your beliefs and values. Eliminate people who are aggressive in their own philosophies and beliefs. They will overpower the knowledge and values of who God is in our lives for status and material gain. If God said it, the promise would come to pass in his time.[51]

A Judas can be an arm's-length friend, a family member, or an acquaintance. These people are trying to represent themselves as our inner circle of friends and family, but they do not add value to our lives. They have a superficial idea of who we are instead of getting to know us more intimately.

Judas wanted the earthly kingdom and riches on this earth. People like that miss the value of sitting and learning new insights from the process of God growing in us. Jesus represents the spiritual kingdom that is greater than the earthly kingdom. It doesn't mean we shouldn't have the nice and comfortable things we desire on this earth. These things are the result of knowing God and receiving his promises. Lack of understanding of the kingdom of God and how it's more valuable than the kingdom on this earth is fruitless.

---

[51] Franklin 2018.

False Alarm Exposed

Betrayal comes when someone is trying to make their expectations of who we are become a reality through alternative narratives. They would rather see us as their created narrative than recognize us and the Christ in us. This reality and the expectations are limiting. They won't recognize the dreams God has shared with us, and they will become a hindrance if we are trying to live up to their expectations instead of God's direction.

Create boundaries, articulate them, and recognize them so other people won't impose their opinions on our lives and our truth, which is revealed by God. If we don't create our own boundaries, people will create them for us.

Turn off the neighbor's alarm, set the record straight in the truth of what God has put in motion, and stop the false alarm. We stop the alarm by recognizing that we are in control of our lives and not subscribing to someone else's narrative of who we are. These impersonal opinions lack consciousness of others and are transferred to us if we care too much about what people think of us. Know your worth and trust God. He is constantly guiding us toward the destiny he set us on this earth.

CHAPTER 5

Rationalism and Mental Incapacitation Limit Mental Freedom

Don't shock our minds. Rationalism incapacitates our intuitive need for "symbolic thinking, and for symbols themselves."[52] According to the scholar Ian Hacking, some dreamers used cyberspace to discuss their dreams in an impersonal way. Are the dreamers serious about getting a true interpretation of their dreams or experimenting with the comments of their artificial associates?[53]

People are searching for relevance and meaning in their lives. They want a place where they can relate to others and feel a sense of belonging to a community. A community doesn't need to have the same beliefs

[52] Hacking 2001.

[53] Hacking 2001.

and values, but common interests and experiences are important. An idealistic viewpoint is significant to create a sense of belonging. The virtual associates provide a space for interpretation of dreams without taking the seriousness of what God is trying to say to the people about their hearts. During the COVID-19 pandemic, misinformation was prevalent on the internet.

Minds Changed

There is peace in mental healing. Mental freedom comes from trusting God and finding peace. This does not mean that we should try to manipulate God through misinterpreting his dreams. Our minds try to override our hearts and their trust in God, and they receive the manifestation of his promise through the dreams and interpretations. Herman Riffel defined the nature of dreams:

> The basic purpose of a dream is to show us the thoughts of our hearts over against the thoughts of our mind. All day long we operate by the thoughts of our mind. When the mind is still, God speaks to our innermost being through the thoughts of our heart in the dream.

> The balance is essential to a fulfilled life.[54]

Sit in the silence of God until he speaks again. God sometimes wants us to find a quiet place to rest. Getting away from the busyness of life, helping others, and being alone with him to receive interpretation of our dreams[55] is essential for growth.

Going to a quiet place gives people an opportunity to get refreshed, be replenished in faith, and understand God's mission for their lives. Miracles should not be rationalized. If they are, the understanding is lost through the lessons God gives us to grow. Lack of understanding what God is speaking to us and providing miracles in our presence through interpretation of our dreams are associated with a person's heart.

Stones in Our Hearts

If the heart of a person is like a stone, they cannot understand why the miracles are happening. Their reasoning steals their dreams. As we get to know God, we have a better idea of where our dreams are taking us. Miracles will manifest what God gives us with the

---

[54] Riffel 1993.

[55] Hinson 1988, Mark 6:31 (NLT).

compassion we display to others who are trying to follow where God is leading them.

Unstoppable action is the freedom to know what God's will is. Being set free is more important than obtaining commercial things. If we are set free to be emotionally charged in our faith and mental capacity, we can pursue the things we desire through the will of God. They will become visible, and whether personal or material, it will all work out.[56] We must let go of the stones in our hearts and trust in God through his dreams and visions. When the stones are removed, our hearts will be joyful with the manifestation of God's dreams and revelation.

What time is it? The concept of time in dreams is not the same as in real life. Prayer changes our destinies, and God answers prayers in His time and in his way.[57] He knows all, he sees all, and he is all-powerful. He makes our dreams, visions, and destinies come true. Outside of sleep, we are working toward the destiny God has destined for us. During sleep, we depart reality and enter our subconsciousness via our dreams. Our dreams provide guidance, self-realization, internal truth, and life in another dimension. God's guidance tells us what is vital in our lives. We must obey his

---

[56] Batterson 2016.

[57] Batterson 2016.

standard of kingdom living, which is presented through his written Word.

There are times when we must get our heads out the clouds and look around. If we live a whimsical life of hoping that everything is a bed of roses, we will be embarrassed or destroyed by the people who are not cognizant of our destinies. Lack of knowledge is destructive to going forward in truth. We must find a balance between dreaming and conscious reality. Faith takes us beyond the immediate reality we might be experiencing. We might be going through controversies, fights, negativity with friends and family, negative media, or struggles with our mental health. These activities are overcome by understanding and holding on to what we know to be true for our lives.

Don't Be Double-Minded

Mental and emotional bondage makes us incapable of seeing what God is saying to us to lead us to our destinies.[58] It keeps us from reaching the expected promises of God that he has provided. We have steadfast faith, but if we don't believe in the dreams and goals God provides us, we are double-minded.

---

[58] Jeremiah 29:11 (NLT).

Double-mindedness stops us from seeing the truth we are trusting in God. His dreams, visions, and truth set us free from the bondage of rationalism.[59] It separates us from the universe around us, and we risk falling into superstition and beliefs that are not of God.[60] Mental and emotional bondage from a cruel society is overcome by believing in a higher being for deliverance. Believe in God and his progress of freedom—no matter how slow or fast the progress. Overcoming incapacitation to our intuitive needs causes mental freedom and will produce success. Prosperity is evident as societies and cultures coalesce and bring people to a higher position of equality and belonging in society.

Overthinking can be overwhelming, but people must realize that it takes trust to rise above mental belligerence. Most individuals want to rationalize their dreams and give them a scientific meaning. Miracles are then rationalized and limited to scientific interpretations. People who dream and remember them tend to ignore the messages of truth God is trying to reveal to them and give more credence to scientific magnifications. These actions are contrary to faith in what they are asking God to reveal. Faith over scientific interpretations is beyond what group dynamics and

---

[59] 2 Corinthians 3:17–18 (KJV).

[60] Gilbert 1985, Corinthians 2 10:5 (NLT).

cultural beliefs have taught. The information in dreams is not reality oriented. They are tied to emotional and unique symbols where the person having the dreams receives the interpretation as correct.[61]

This view of rationalizing dreams scientifically dulls the senses to our soul connection to God. The dullness happens when God is explained as anything other than the supernatural loving Creator who guides his people to their destinies through dreams and visions.

61 Montague, Krippner, and Vaughan 2002, 178.

CHAPTER 6

The Language of Symbols

Eliminate confusion by understanding the difference in earthly views other than God's truth. Scientifically, symbolism is a Jungian construct.[62] A person will look for an answer to their dreams in nonspiritual ways and not take the interpretations seriously. They will relate to an understanding of their dreams as if interpretation is the same as astrology or palm reading. According to Ian Hacking, "Features of dreaming are shared by all people ... utilizing a universal symbolic system."[63]

Dreams are relevant to our current lives.[64] Scholars have proven with scientific data that precognitive

[62] Gilbert 1985, 8, Batterson 2016.
[63] Hacking 2001, 245.
[64] Krippner 1990.

dreaming is a "universal human experience."[65] There are ways to determine and know when a dream or vision is from God and recognize false messages in dreams and visions. The interpretation is personal, and people will know the truth from false revelation. It takes a close relationship with God to know his voice. We can build two-way communication like we do with anyone else on earth.

The language of symbols is developed by building relationships. Relationships are a treasure.[66] Trust doesn't happen overnight. It must be developed as we spend time with a person before we know they are speaking to us. We get to know people personally and intimately when we spend time with them and listen to their voices. A shepherd is always in the field, protecting, leading, and guiding their sheep.[67] The sheep know his voice and follow him. When we haven't spoken or heard someone's voice for a while, can we recognize the person's voice? If we love them and haven't heard their voice in a while, we will recognize it right away. We will passionately be drawn to them and want to hear from them again.

Boundaries are crucial to understanding what God is saying. The most important thing in life is loving

[65] Ullman 1990.

[66] Franklin 2018, 17.

[67] John 10:27 (NLT).

God, self, and others. Loving someone in our dreams can manifest on a conscious level. Loving our neighbors in our dreams and on a conscious level determines the outcome of what God is trying to show us in our dreams. Set boundaries. People get turned off by someone competing with us for our love in a negative way. This is very toxic. It doesn't mean they have stopped loving us, but it might represent their unwillingness to love us as much as they want to.

Make a conscious decision to love someone unconditionally—no matter who tries to compete for our love. God's love will prevail, and everyone will win. He gets the glory. Truth wins over a lie that might arise in the competition for love. Praise God and know he will continue to bless what he said he would do as we continue our journeys in life. Don't give up on the ones loved—and press through the obstacles to get a stronger relationship.

Dulled and constrained emotions impair faith and trust in God. Del Tar stated, "The language of faith is the language of symbols."[68] Suppressing the emotional inner selves muffles the language of faith. Faith in the interpretation of the symbols must come from within as a person understands or someone interprets their dreams in a personal way. This means that we personally will agree with the interpretation and know

---

[68] Tarr 1985.

that it is from God. The lack of feelings of identity and belonging are eliminated when truth is revealed, and maturity and growth ensue.

Victory in Our Dreams

It was dark like the deep void of an abyss. A shadow came and choked the dreamer. The dark shadow, looking like a human covered with dark black muck, resembled the darkness with a head, two arms, and two legs. One hand gripped the dreamer's neck. It wasn't a squeeze like we would squeeze fruit for ripeness. The pressure was steady and intended to bring harm to the dreamer and remove her last breath. She kept straining through the choke, singing "God Is So Amazing," and with her left arm kept reaching to the sky. She repeatedly shouted the name of Jesus.

The choking didn't deter her from singing and calling out the name of Jesus. The blackened shadow figure left. Shortly after this encounter, it came back with two other monsters. One was standing to the left, and the other one was standing over her head and gripping it. Her head was slung back. She looked up and the monster opened her mouth wide in an unnatural way. It was trying to enter through her mouth.

She again cried out singing the song "God Is So

Amazing." Her voice strained through the choking, and she was singing the same stanza. "God Is So Amazing" rose from within. She started to push up with her left arm and pushed past the strain as she sang loudly. Her arm was pushing back at the apparition, and her mouth was pulled open wider. The demon tried to choke out the song, and the other one tried to enter her mouth. They tried to stop her from using her voice to worship God. The more they tried, the harder and louder she sang and pushed up to the heavens. She awakened from the sleep state, in the same form as if she had pushed from the subconscious level to an awakened state. Her left arm was pushed toward heaven, and she heard herself singing loudly "God Is So Amazing" again.

The dreamer jumped exuberantly from her bed and praised God. She had broken through from the subconscious to the conscious reality. At that moment, her dream became the reality of truth. The barrier had been broken. This was an answer to a prayer. She had written down a list of goals and was asking God for eight days if he was pleased with them. She was going through relationship turmoil with meddling neighbors, someone she was deeply concerned with, and lying spirits. Fasting and praying was her focus as she was setting boundaries and goals for her near future. The devil tried to send distractions to stop her from speaking what they believed would come to pass in the name of Jesus who lives in her heart.

There are times when we must stop praying and start praising God for his promise and what he is going to do. We must have a balance of praising and praying toward our end point. Pray and then praise, and then pray, and then praise. After we stir up the faith within us and see the revelations of our dreams, it's time to start praising God avidly. Start praising God for answering our dream interpretation request and inquiries of direction and guidance.

How can we hear what someone is saying if we are constantly talking or if others are constantly talking around us? Stop the chatter and idle talk. Two-way conversations are so satisfying when we get on the same page with each other. It's even more satisfying when we hear from God and want to bask in his presence and never let go. Put on our listening ears in the spirit, have faith, and hear what he has to say.

Relationships can be satisfying when we recognize the Christ in each other and execute his loving ways. The most important thing to do is to get up and act on his promises for our lives. Our dreams are a mechanism in which God can accomplish great things in us if we let him. God's dreams come to pass when they manifest in our awakened lives.

CHAPTER 7

Dreaming is Personal

Don't be hard of hearing. Stop and listen. Prayer is a form of speaking to God from a human standpoint.[69] We approach prayer as communication with God and have a yearning to hear back from him. God can speak to us by sending the answers back through dreams and visions that are intimately revealed to our innermost being by his Holy Spirit. The relationship requires two-way communication.

Praying and dreaming are synonymous with one another. The Holy Spirit of God illuminates our dreams and visions. We call this "imagination on steroids" or "immovable faith." The two actions are so closely connected in most people's minds that one suggests

---

[69] Jeremiah 29:11–12 (AMPC).

the other. G. William Domhoff's research reveals that dreaming is "a cognitively mature imagination system."[70] Faith is something where the world thinks we are delusional to dream and believe in our dreams. Faith brings our dreams to pass as God orchestrates the journey.

Getting connected is exhilarating. Mark Batterson defines a personal connection with God through prayer and faith as an interpersonal relationship that is always growing.[71] The sacredness of the symbolic dream revelation expands our imaginary potential and faith to bring to pass from our subconscious a conscious level of reality. Dreams help us "circle the goals God wants you to go after, the promises God's wants you to claim, and the dreams God wants you to pursue."[72]

Dreams help us learn how to overcome obstacles that present themselves to us and need to be resolved. They help us prepare for events that are coming up in our lives and give us peace to accept the upcoming experiences. Once we understand our dreams, we begin to open ourselves up to healing from emotional and mental bondage. We understand what is holding us back from being successful in our lives, relationships, communications with others, and belonging to a society

[70] Domhoff 2018, 357.

[71] Batterson 2016, 12.

[72] Batterson 2016, 30.

that encourages us to grow in our circumstances—whether they are positive or not.

People who want to grow in their relationships must spend time intimately with one another to get to know each other and expand their relationship. The "free love or casual love"[73] of today adds no value to long-term relationships because love is defined and converted to material things.[74] There is nothing memorable about doing your thing without a true connection to someone. When you have a deeper connection with someone, you connect on a deeper level and bond in a more intimate way. Love God and yourself—and then love others. In a culture where dreams are important, it is greater to remember them[75] because we understand that love is coming out from the inside.

Dreams are remembered more frequently when people feel reverence for them and acknowledge the importance of dreams and visions in their lives. Everyone does not remember their dreams, and if they do, they do not find it important to understand what the dreams and visions mean if they are not interesting or disturbing enough to seek interpretations.

Some scholars acknowledge that dreams and visions are a part of everyday life from a scientific

---

[73] Franklin 2018.

[74] Ibid.

[75] Ullman 1990.

perspective[76]. The spiritual point of view in relation to this worldview is basically the same since they are both a part of daily living. Distinguishing the truth from falsehoods is determined through the background and understanding of the dreamer.

Be delighted and know dreams and visions are revelations for our growth and success and for others to follow. Dreams gratify the individual and society.[77] They are responsive to beliefs, values, ethnicities, and family dynamics. The family dynamics passes down the oral history of family members who are sensitive to the lineage of visionaries and dreamers.

The lineage of dreams and visionaries in our families might come from oral stories of different characteristics of the familial dreamers. Superstitions are intertwined with these historical interactions, and cultural beliefs discern the truth from falsehoods. The dreamers' cultural beliefs and family dynamics incorporate the value of a person who can see into the spiritual world as a blessing and insight into God's guidance through dreams and visions. Folklore helps us understand that multiple societies comprehend what it means to be born "under the veil"[78] or as the seventh child. This seventh child could be a stand-alone number of children or

[76] Cushway 1992.
[77] Krippner 1990, 194.
[78] Rich 1976.

one of more than ten children in a household. They understand the promises of God throughout their family dynamics from bondage to freedom.

Timing and legacy are everything in our dream and visionary transition. The lineage of dreamers and visionaries in the Bible brought about God's promises in the Old Testament through types and shadows of Jesus. New Testament revelations are where our Lord and Savior Jesus fulfilled biblical promises in God's timing. As Christians, we have Jesus in us and his Holy Spirit to bring his truth to us. A mental and emotional enlargement of the world we live in[79] is understanding where we came from and how our identities are moving forward in life for God's glory. It includes our interactions with people who do not encourage growth in our lives. They are trying to figure out their own lives and overshadow us with their issues instead of resolving themselves. They try to highlight what we are doing wrong to hide their own insecurities and failures. Watch who's communicating with you—and whether they are gossiping, making idle talk, or sharpening one another.

The gift of prophecy should not be taken lightly. Interpretation should go beyond what we are doing, and the interpretation can eliminate any issue we might

[79] Maxwell 2009, 10.

not be confronting. Use wisdom to evaluate prophetical dreams. They will come to pass—whether we believe them or not. It might be a moment of warning to keep us from going in the wrong direction. The dream might be a promise supported by God's written Word that is a desire in their heart. If we choose not to believe in our dreams, we will eventually put the dream in the back of our minds. When it does come to pass, it's like believing we are having a déjà vu moment.

CHAPTER 8

Dreams are Intimate Encounters

The transparency of God reveals his inner truth. Interpreting dreams is Gods matter. Interpreting dreams belongs to him and starts with us. It is essential to yield to God for understanding and interpretation.[80] Dreams are the literal mixed with symbolism and need to be interpreted accordingly.[81] God is in control and does not interfere with who we reveal our dreams to. We are in control of who we reveal our dreams to and for receiving interpretation in our spirit as valid. Try the spirit and see if it is God. "Listen," he said, and try and understand.[82] If what comes out of our hearts is defiled, we will know the truth—and it will set us free.

[80] Genesis 40:8 (NLT).
[81] Hamon 2000, 105, Riffel 1993, 163.
[82] Matthew 15:10 (NLT).

Repentance is important for taking action and turning away from our unwholesome ways.

Believing that a dream interpretation as one-dimensional is a fallacy. Most dream interpretations are for the dreamer and the visionary. Interpretation comes in layers.[83] Dreams might be helpful for someone else and will be revealed by God as such through a dream or vision. Only God knows the hearts and minds of humans.

We can learn from the experiences and the lessons that lead to growth and maturity. God revealed the culmination of Joseph's destiny through the dream he shared with his family and lifetime journey. Joseph was so excited about a dream God gave him that he told his brothers and father about the dream right away. When we share our dreams with our closest family members, beware of the spirit of envy coming upon siblings and other family members. Telling others about our dreams opens the door to their emotions and mental capacity. This open door won't be good if our family support and friends are superficial.

Joseph was a dreamer, and as his dreams manifested into reality, his success in life came to fruition. He chose to forgive his family for treating him so cruelly. He understood that sharing his dream with them caused

[83] Green 2012.

envy in their hearts. Their jealousy about what God was doing for him created his humble beginnings.[84] God blessed Joseph to interpret dreams for others during his life. Dreams are literal and metaphorical, and success comes in interpretation by using Gods wisdom and practical wisdom.[85] Joseph went through his wilderness experience due to his family's manipulation, lying, and animosity toward their brother's future success, which he shared with them[86] from his dream.

People close to us won't necessarily share our enthusiasm and love for what God is doing in our lives, and they might try to snuff out our voices. They will try to create a narrative about who we are instead of who God has created us to be. Those who are hovering around us at arm's length will do anything to keep us from expressing what God is doing in our lives. Don't worry because our most intimate friends and family will try to understand and support us in what we share with them about our dreams. We don't always have to share what God gives us with anyone. What is revealed and given in secret will come to light no matter what we do.

Cut out the noise. It is designed to distract and will cause a collision. Some things are not revealed or

---

[84] Franklin 2018.

[85] Genesis 41:1–57.

[86] Genesis 37:22.

delivered except through fasting and prayer. Fasting is a form of denying cultured things and consecrating ourselves to God for his holy interpretation.

Traditionally, food was the thing to consecrate from because this is what Daniel, and his friends did when they were put into bondage to serve a king from another culture. Fasting in the New Testament was the social process of denying food and doing certain activities during the time of fasting. It was a way for the high priest to approach God the Father in prayer and supplication on behalf of his people.

The death and resurrection of Jesus gives us an opportunity to understand that he is our High Priest.[87] He is making an intercession on our behalf. In his name is how we pray today to the Father, and the fasting goes beyond denying the bodily functions that were prior to salvation through Jesus. It is understanding that Jesus shed his blood for us to come to the Father in prayer and stand in agreement with Jesus that our prayers are answered. The veil was ripped open from top to bottom.[88] The minds that were blinded are opened to the knowledge and wisdom of God. Truth is now revealed in our hearts and souls.

Jesus made a way when he died on the cross with

---

87 Hebrews 10:20–22 (NLT).

88 Luke 23:45–46 (KJV).

his death and resurrection. Belief in the name of Jesus and his resurrection power manifests miracles. Eyes are opened, and minds are set free.[89] Most people fast symbolically to understand something that has been revealed to us as truth. Make it personal by getting the understanding that Jesus is our High Priest. By the blood shed at Calvary, he is the one who cleanses us from our sins and gives us an opportunity to come to the throne of grace in prayer and supplication. Be humble and get to know him personally. His name and power break bondage and give deliverance.[90]

It's all right to be an enduring learner; this action elevates us to our destinies. Daniel and his friends had to learn every aspect of literature and the wisdom of another culture due to their bondage and to be successful.[91] The challenge was to keep their beliefs and faith in how they represented God in their lives before their bondage.

Today, people might get caught up in their daily lives and be engulfed in the routines of eating, sleeping, working, and being immersed in social media and social activities. These cultural actions will keep us too busy to hear what God is trying to tell us or provide direction for our journeys. Collective action prior to

---

[89] 2 Corinthians 3:14–17 (KJV).

[90] 2 Corinthians 3: 17–18, 4:18 (KJV).

[91] Daniel 1.

the interpretation biblically in the past was to avoid eating certain foods that we were not brought up on in our beliefs and values.[92] Over time, it becomes apparent that we must hold onto the beliefs and faith in how we represent God in society. Once a person becomes a believer in Christ Jesus, they learn every aspect of the Bible that they can understand. God provides the wisdom and knowledge to grow.

To overcome the mental and emotional thoughts that could obstruct us from hearing from God, we must find a significant thing that we can deny as a form of fasting. Noteworthy mechanisms could be telephones or media. It is difficult to stop talking on the phone, watching TV, and engaging in social media. Try ten days denying use of television, social media, radio, and communications that are not uplifting our spirits. There are so many other activities that can be accomplished besides these vices. For example, reading is one such activity.

Watching television takes away from taking time to be on our knees and praying to God for the answers we have been looking for from him in a special way. Social media is addictive because it tries to substitute our sense of belonging with bonding with people superficially for the satisfaction of not being alone. Talking on the phone

[92] Daniel 1:15–17 (NLT).

every day to someone does not create a real connection. A balance of face-to-face interaction with phone calls, emails, or social media helps build a solid relationship.

Face-to-face conversations are the best way to make the bonding process stick. Speaking on the phone daily is no substitute for face-to-face conversations. Some people do not really want to have face-to-face conversations to create personal connections. They might be using a person to emotionally unload on if they don't feel close enough to share their intimate feelings. A quiet, sensitive person is compassionate and will listen to complaints without judgments. The person who wants to talk every day wants control over the people they are speaking with, and they will only deposit overwhelming emotions when they should be getting professional help. They are dumping their emotional baggage on the other person in a careless and haphazard manner, expecting them to handle it without showing any intimacy or consideration.

These activities are distractions from what God is doing in our lives. He is the one who shares the deep things in our hearts through our dreams and visions. The deep things are connected to our innermost being and our communities. God gives us the special ability to interpret the meanings of our visions and dreams. He gives us understanding of literature and wisdom and tells us how to move toward the destiny he has prepared for us. When we have a job to do, it is the same job as the other prophets in a close community. We are not alone.

Prophets know each other and vibe together to give God the glory. The interpretation of our dreams could come from a special person who knows us and cares about us intimately, such as a friend, pastor, or family member. Someone who is used by God in a prophetical ministry or fivefold ministry could also help interpret our dreams. Harmon agrees that "those with a strong prophetic anointing often demonstrate a supernatural ability to discern the meaning of dreams."[93]

God will speak to them directly and provide confirmation in our spirits of what he has already spoken. The mysterious secret treasures of the heart are not easily received by people through dreams, sometimes due to denial, and work must be done to get to the revelation. Yield to God for understanding and interpretation.[94] Dreams can have a current meaning or a meaning that will assist in healings or warnings from past issues. They also reveal future events. Visions have current and future meanings that will flow into the destinies that our creative potential will manifest.[95]

---

[93] Hamon 2000, Daniel 1:17.

[94] Genesis 40:8 (NLT).

[95] Krippner 1990, Green 2012.

CHAPTER 9

Write Down Your Dreams and Visions

Strength and faith are reinforced through writing down what God gives us and dating it. The prophets in the Bible dated their dreams. It's important to date our dreams in our journals. Prophets and people with the spirit of prophecy and visions make a habit of documenting their dreams and visions. Be disciplined and write down your dreams. You can also video them or record them. The Holy Spirit will provide interpretations of your dreams and visions and explain how God illustrates his points. The person will understand God's view of the things they are secretly harboring in their hearts and minds. These things are kept hidden by a protective layer in the heart—or deliberately desired to act upon—but they have not due to moral conflicts.

God knows the innermost things of our hearts.

While we document our dreams, we should also wait for an answer from God.[96] In the silence, God will tell us to wait patiently. We must quiet our spirits, listen, and pay attention to the dreams he shares with us as we ponder what he shared in our quiet space. Be attentive to direction and guidance. We might mess up if we don't fully understand what our dreams are telling us, but we must keep going until we get the complete picture.

To understand the symbols and meanings of our dreams, we need discipline, obedience, faith, and understanding. We also must be patient and set boundaries. If we have faith in what he tells us, we will understand how to pursue the life of the dream. If we are constantly talking to God and not respecting him by listening for an answer, we will miss out on the direct answer. Make documenting the dreams a habit and seek God for interpretation. The first line of defense in understanding comes from the Bible. God's Holy Spirit will reveal a scripture to you to understand the cultural beliefs, values, and changes in culture in the New Testament with the life, death, and resurrection of Christ Jesus. The interpretation of our dreams belongs to God. Give God a chance to speak—and trust him by writing down the promise of the dream.

Writing and discipline bring success. Follow

[96] Habakkuk 2:2–4, 20 (NLT).

this lead. Upon waking, write down the dream as soon as possible. Date and timestamp it. We can also electronically record our dreams. Keep a journal and a pen or pencil on your nightstand or an electronic device that is easily available for recording. If a person doesn't write down the dream upon waking, they tend to forget it. Write down as much as you remember.[97] Leave it for a while and go back to the dream. If you remember more details, write them down. Review what you wrote down when you are fully awake.

Pray for an interpretation of the dream. If the interpretation was not given directly upon inquiring of God, we will be guided to the right person who can assist in the interpretation. Don't be nonchalant and ask someone who is not close to you. Social media tends to give people a false sense of others. Social media does not necessarily present the real person. It presents a narrative of someone, and if this is all we rely on to get to know a person, we are falling for a façade that has been created artificially. When we are intimate with someone, it is more than a social media show. Media narratives and shows only represent a part of the person without any depth.

Be obedient to your boundaries and go forward in reaching out for an interpretation of what God is trying

---

[97] Montague, Krippner, and Vaughn 2002.

to tell you. You are healing from the inside out. Our faith keeps us on track to know that God will reveal his truth in his time and when we need strength to grow. Don't let a lack of knowledge prevent you from getting to the truth. This truth will come to light when the discernment of your understanding is released through prayer and supplication to God. The hope of your calling will manifest beyond faith[98] in your dreams and visions from him.

---

[98] Ephesians 1:8, 17–18.

CHAPTER 10

Having Faith and Confidence in Our Dreams Creates Growth

Don't be scared. Keep pushing through. The scariest thing to do is be vulnerable to the world of who you are and not feel protection in our times of vulnerability. The world can be cruel and unforgiving. We can feel confidence that God is the greatest protector in our lives. He wants to commune with us continually, and a great way to do so is when we are asleep, resting, or consciously using our gift of spiritual sight.

Sleep is the quietest time and another condition we can be in to hear his voice. Once we learn to hear his voice, we are in a position in life, conscious or sleep, to know his voice and loving-kindness. Our intuition never stops working. We sometimes ignore the nudges of intuition and second-guess what is being said. We are not alone, and our friends and family know our personalities and can support our visions and dreams.

Stay balanced and be renewed daily. Our bodies, while asleep, are regenerating for another day. We are moving forward to do what we believe he wants us to do. A community of loved ones and friends helps us stay grounded in life. They give us balance. We must set and adhere to our boundaries to maintain that balance. It prevents us from overthinking things and not giving our gifts enough respect to grow spiritually and effectively.

A flower grows in stages from a seed in the ground to fully blooming. God is with us throughout the growth process. He is our strength and flexibility. The flexibility is needed to provide function to other parts of our lives. Dreams help us in all issues. Out of the bulging bicep, the stem and bud show up first. As biceps prepare your arm for movement, God's dreams prepare us for movement toward a balanced end. The symbolism of the petals manifesting ever so slowly to show the beauty of the flower shows us that, if we are patient in our process of interpretation and conscious manifestation, we will see the beauty of what our lives are becoming through our dreams. The nutrition from the ground to the seed to the bud gives the flower the strength to push through, knowing there is more to the flower than meets the eye. Not all flowers bloom, but if we are obedient and continue moving toward success, ours will bloom all the way.

Darkness tries to distract us, but if we keep our eyes on the growth of the flower, like the growth of the manifestations of his promises in our lives, they will manifest to its fullness in God's time. Men and women have different views of the growth and beauty of the flower. Everyone will get there individually and intimately with Jesus on their side. A flower will reach its full potential.

Men and women may interpret the symbolic elements of dreams differently. Men may focus on one aspect of the dream as a way to understand the journey, while women may see the different chapters of their lives as interconnected with their relationships. Each person interprets their individual journey on a unique level, even if they initially have a common goal. The rewards they receive will be based on their efforts to fulfill their divine purpose, leading to potentially different experiences and methods of understanding.

Men's level of fullness in progression might come at a different level than women. They might not see the pollen in the flower and the shape it is woven into by God from a woman's viewpoint. Perception depends on the view and growth of the pedals to the onlooker.

Women might see the beauty of the pollen and know the hope of the calling before them as unique to them. It emerges from the growth and magnitude of the petals. Yellow is trimmed with pure white. The pollen is like strategic warfare that will bring about deliverance from and victory against the devil. The white and yellow represent Jesus and his purity and holiness. The bluish-purple is the sovereignty and royalty of God. It is the self-government and promises as we are fully covered to receive what he has prepared for us. We are wrapped in his provisions and presence.

Tears are turned to joy. A flower needs rain to grow. The good sometimes comes with the bad.[99] It is beneficial to cleanse all the unclean things in our bodies by weeping. Out of our tears will be joy in understanding what God is intimately speaking to us. If we are required to speak in public, but we are too timid to do the speech, we can find confidence in the dreams God gives us. Our hearts will still pump fast, and our legs will still wobble. Our ears will be drumming to the heartbeat of our nervousness. Take a breath, take a step, and go forward—and God will do the rest. Trust God always. We will have multiple dreams, but we must be able to distinguish the dreams as coming from God and needing interpretation. Not all dreams appear as

[99] Isaiah 45:7 (NLT).

direct as the one noted in the dreamer who was called to preaching in the streets.

No matter what our dreams are, acting on what we believe helps propel us to our destinies through faith. God knows our personalities and his plans for our lives. When we feed our souls with the Word of God and uplifting songs, we connect with his plan for our mission in life on this earth. We cannot let anyone, or anything choke out our voices. Our boundaries are real and need to be unmovable. Our voices will manifest on a conscious level what is birthed in our innermost being in our sleep and subconscious. Trials and obstacles will try to stop the manifestation of our dreams, but we have the nutrition of God's Word and his iconic voice through the dreams and visions that guide us to victory.

Mental and physical control are characteristics, and one cannot move without the other. Emotional control—from the innermost being through the revelation of our dreams—can set us free. We are victorious individuals, and we can stand our ground in victory.

There is a tour of a facility in an unknown place. To the right, there is a clear window from the top to the bottom of the wall. Outside the window, as the dreamer orients herself to the place, it is not on earth. It appears to be another planet or a moon. Everything is white.

The window is arched, and the hallway seems to be circular—but only half of it has been revealed.

The narrator is speaking of a place for the dreamer to be brought for action. The dreamer is treated as a dignitary with military skill and prominence. As they approach a room on the left, everything is white. There is a seat the dreamer is supposed to sit in. The large robotic chair has a suit to climb into. It looks like a space suit without the helmet. Two arms are straight out, and two legs are bent in the chair. She is familiarized with the suit and its purpose.

The narrator explains how the dreamer is supposed to operate the equipment. She is guided to sit in the suit and lift her right leg and then slam it down on a foot pedal, which will cause a large explosion outside the window. The explosion is large, but she can't see what is being blown up. The dreamer awakens.

Her arms stretch toward the ceiling, and her legs are bent. She thinks, *I hope my granddaughter didn't see that.* It is early in the morning, and the granddaughter might have woken up and seen her grandmother doing something odd. The granddaughter is in the room across from her grandmother's bedroom, but she is still asleep.

Maybe it's time to teach the next generation of dreamers. The subconscious has broken through to the conscious again. The future is being revealed.

Bibliography

Batterson, Mark. 2016. *The Circle Maker: Praying Circles Around Your Biggest Dreams and Greatest Fears.* Austin, Texas: Fedd & Company.

Branam, Chris M. 2023. *Slave Codes.* Central Arkansan Library Systems (CALS), accessed January 2024. https://encyclopediaofarkansas.net/entries/slave-codes-5054/.

Cirlot, J. E. 2001, 1971, 1962. *A Dictionary of Symbols,* second edition. Translated from Spanish by Jack Sage. London: Taylor & Francis e-Library, Routledge & Kegan Paul Ltd.

Crank, Nicole. 2020. *Goal Getters: 5 Steps to Finally Getting What You Want.* Avail, The Art of Leadership Publishing Company.

Cushway, Delia and Sewell, Robyn. 1992. *Counselling with Dreams and Nightmares.* Newbury Park, California: SAGE Publications.

Domhoff, G. William. 2018. "Dreaming is an Intensified Form of Mind-Wandering." *The Oxford Handbook of Spontaneous Thought*, Kieran C. R. Fox and Kalina Christoff. New York: Oxford University Press.

Flanagan, Owen J. 2000. *Dreaming souls: Sleep, Dreams, and the Evolution of the Conscious Mind.* New York: Oxford University Press.

Fox, Kieran C. R., and Kalina Christoff. 2018. *The Oxford Handbook of Spontaneous Thought: Mind-Wandering, Creativity, and Dreaming.* Vol. xvi. New York, NY: Oxford University Press.

Franklin, Jentezen. 2018. *Love Like You've Never Been Hurt: Hope, Healing, and the Power of an Open Heart.* Edited by Cherise Franklin and A. J. Gregory. Bloomington, Minnesota: Chosen, a division of Baker Publishing Group.

Gilbert, Marvin G. and Brock, Raymond T., ed. 1985. *The Holy Spirit and Counseling.* Peabody, MA: Hendrickson Publishers.

Green, Jackie L. Bishop Dr. 2012. *Vanguard of Visions and Dreams: The Lifestyle and Warfare of God's Visionary.* Bloomington, Indiana: AuthorHouse.

Hacking, Ian. 2001. "Dreams in Place." Summer: 245–260.

Hamon, Jane. 2000. *Dreams and Visions: Understanding Your Dreams and How God Can Use Them to Speak to You Today.* Ventura, California: Regal Books.

Hinson, William H. 1988. *Reshaping the Inner You: Being Transformed by the Power of God's Love.* New York: Guideposts, Harper and Row.

Krippner, Stanley, PhD, ed. 1990. *Dreamtime and Dreamwork: Decoding the Language of the Night.* Los Angeles: Jeremy P. Tarcher.

Maxwell, John C. 2009. *How Successful People Think: Change Your Thinking, Change Your Life.* Orange, California: Yates & Yates, LLP.

Montague, Ullman, Krippner, Stanley, and Vaughan, Alan. 2002. *Dream Telepathy: Scientific Experiments in the Supernatural.* Charlottesville, VA: Hampton Roads Publishing Company.

Murphy, Joseph, PhD, DD. 2008. *The Power of Your Subconscious Mind.* New York: Prentice Hall Press.

Prince, Derek. 1993. *The Spirit-Filled Believer's Handbook.* Altamonte Springs, Florida: Creation House Strang Communications Company.

Rich, Carroll Y. 1976. "Born with the Veil: Black Folklore in Louisiana." *The Journal of American Folklore* (American Folklore Society) 89 (No. 353): 328–331.

Riffel, Herman H. 1993. *Dream Interpretation: A Biblical Understanding.* Shippensburg, PA: Destiny Image Publishers.

Tarr, Del. 1985. "The Role of the Holy Spirit in Interpersonal Relations." *The Holy Spirit and Counseling,* Marvin G & Brock, Raymond T. Gilbert. Peabody, Massachusetts: Hendrickson Publishers.

Ullman, Montague. 1990. "Guidelines for Teaching Dreamwork." Edited by Stanley Krippner, 122–133. Los Angeles: Jeremy P. Tarcher.

New Release Now Available

"I Hear Your Voice" by Paula Yolandé

Printed in the United States
by Baker & Taylor Publisher Services